A HO

HORRID HENRY'S
CRAZY
CREATURES

Francesca Simon spent her
...ildhood on the beach in California, and
...en went to Yale and Oxford Universities
...o study medieval history and li...rature.
...he now lives in London with h...r family.
...e has written over fifty books a...d won the
...hildren's Book of the Year in...08 at the
...laxy British Book Awards fo...*orrid Henry
and the Abominable Sr*......*an.*

librar

Tony Ross is one o...ain's
best-known illustrators......many
picture books to his n...ue...as well as
line drawings for mar...a...ction titles.
He lives in ...ales.

For a complete list of
Horrid Henry titles, visit

www.horridhenry.co.uk

or

www.orionbooks.co.uk

A HORRID FACTBOOK

HORRID HENRY'S
CRAZY
CREATURES

Francesca Simon
Illustrated by Tony Ross

Orion
Children's Books

First published in Great Britain in 2015
by Orion Children's Books
an imprint of Hachette Children's Books
a division of Hodder & Stoughton Ltd
Carmelite House
50 Victoria Embankment
London EC4Y 0DZ
An Hachette UK Company

1 3 5 7 9 10 8 6 4 2

Text © Francesca Simon 2015
Illustrations © Tony Ross 2015

ISBN 978 1 4440 1444 0

The moral right of Francesca Simon and Tony Ross
to be identified as author and illustrator
of this work has been asserted.

Facts compiled by Sally Byford

A catalogue record for this book is available
from the British Library.

Printed in Great Britain by
Clays Ltd, St Ives plc

www.horridhenry.co.uk
www.orionchildrensbooks.com
www.hachette.co.uk

CONTENTS

Hello from Henry

Hey gang!

This new book is all about creepy creatures like my worm brother, and my evil enemy frog-face Margaret, and batty Miss Battle-Axe and...
Oh.
CRAZY creatures.
Sorry!

This book is all about the *other* kind of crazy creatures, like killer mice, beardie-weirdie pigs, sneaky snakes, dracula ants, and brain-eating, blood-sucking, poo-loving birds — EWWWWWWWWWWW.

And that's just the beginning. Thrill your friends! Gross out your parents with all these hideously horrid fun facts. Wow. I've just had the best idea for some new pets...

Tee Hee.

Henry

FUNNY
FAMILIES

When baby **blue whales** are born, their tail pops out first and their head last. The baby has to swim straight to the surface of the water to breathe before it **drowns**.

All bears, including **pandas** and **polar bears**, give birth to **tiny** cubs, as small as an adult's clenched fist. They weigh only about one kilogram, the same as a big **bag of pasta**.

Giraffes begin life with a **crash landing**! As their mums give birth **standing up**, the newborns have to **fall** around **two metres** to the ground – the height of a tall man.

Too bad that didn't happen to Margaret ... Tee hee.

Elephant babies take 22 months – almost **two years** – to develop inside their mothers before they are born. That's the **longest** time of any mammal.

Alligators build a mound of rotting plants to keep their **35–50 eggs** safe. As the babies hatch, Mum carefully digs them out and carries them to water **in her mouth**.

On 29 November 2004 in the UK, Tia the **Neapolitan mastiff** gave birth to a record-breaking litter of **24 puppies** – nine females and 15 males. Her record is still unbroken.

Bornean bearded pigs are born beardless in the rainforests of southeast Asia. But it isn't long before the piglets follow in their proud parents' footsteps. They start growing **big bushy beards** at only **five weeks** old!

In south-west Africa, male **Namaqua sandgrouse** have to fly up to **80 km** a day to find a drink for their babies. They soak their chests with water and fly back so their young can drink by sucking on their wet feathers.

Emperor penguin dads are truly devoted. Mum produces **a single precious egg**, then leaves Dad to protect it by balancing it on his feet for **two whole months**. He can't move, he can't eat and he can't let the egg touch the ground, otherwise it will freeze and crack, killing the chick inside.

Thick-billed murres from Canada and Russia don't build nests. Instead, Mum lays a single egg on a **narrow cliff ledge** and builds a wall around it, using pebbles cemented together **with poo**. The egg hatches in 30–35 days – unless, of course, it's already rolled into the sea.

When **baby birds** beg for food, they display the bright colours of their **wide-open mouths**. Scientists think parents give more food to the chicks with the **brightest mouths** because it shows that they are the healthiest and most likely to survive.

Cuckoos are **terrible parents**. Mum lays her eggs in another bird's nest, then flies away **never to return**, leaving her chicks to be fed and raised by surrogate parents.

Arowana fish dads are **mouthbrooders**. This means they carry their 100 or so babies around in their mouths to protect them. Sometimes the babies are allowed out to explore, but at the end of playtime Dad gathers **every single one of them** into his mouth again.

In **Darwin's frog** families, dads look after their eggs by swallowing them and keeping them safe in a **handy throat pocket**. The tadpoles hatch while they are still inside him, and **jump out of their father's mouth** as fully-formed little frogs.

I wonder if that's how Margaret became a frog-face?

Female **seahorses** can produce as many as 2,000 eggs at a time. After that it's over to Dad, who keeps them in a **pouch** on his front. The **baby seahorses** grow inside Dad's pouch until he squeezes them out a few weeks later.

Caecilians are amphibians that look like snakes or worms. Adult caecilians eat insects and lizards, but their babies survive by **eating their mum's skin**. They gobble it up. Mum grows it again over the next few days, and then they eat it all up again. Tasty!

BATTY
BIRDS

Egyptian plovers are known as **crocodile birds** because they eat the insects that live on a crocodile's skin. They get **inside** a crocodile's **open mouth** to clean up scraps of food that are left on its teeth.

Shrikes are small British birds that are **fierce hunters**. They catch large insects and small mammals, then **hang** their dead bodies on **sharp thorns**. This is because they don't have claws, so having their kill hanging there makes it easier for them to **tear their food** into mouth-sized pieces.

Great tits usually eat insects and seeds, but they can **turn nasty**. There's a group in Hungary which has been seen hunting bats down in caves during bad winters, wrenching them from their roosts, and cracking open their skulls to **feast on their brains**.

Hmm. Wonder if a great tit could be tempted by a wormy-worm?

Other birds that turn into **blood-suckers** when seeds are in short supply are the **vampire finches** of South America. They peck at the backs of large seabirds until the **blood** starts to flow, then lap up the blood. The seabirds barely seem to notice.

If you think that's disgusting, the **snowy sheathbills** from the Antarctic are really horrible. They eat almost anything they can find – including **penguin poo**!

Arctic skuas are often compared to **pirates** because they steal most of their food from other birds in mid-air. They attack terns and puffins, forcing them to drop their food, and sometimes even gang up in groups to **bully** their victims.

If you see sea birds with white and grey wings nesting on a cliff – watch out, they could be **fulmars**. Don't get too close or they'll think you're going to hurt their chicks and **vomit** all over you.

I've already told Stuck-up Steve, fulmars love people.

Adélie penguins live together in groups on the rocky Antarctic coastline, building their nests and lining them with small rocks. Sounds like one big happy family – until you hear that some penguins have been spotted **stealing rocks** from their neighbours' nests!

Can you believe it? **Crows** are **clever**! Scientists have been amazed to see crows make **tools**. They make **hooks** from twigs to poke grubs out of trees, and **sharp instruments** from leaves to dig insects out of small places.

In Africa, strange-looking long-legged **secretary birds** stalk mice, frogs, birds and snakes. They use their strong legs and feet to **stamp** their prey to death.

According to research done in 1998 by scientists at the University of Chicago, **sleeping birds dream**. It is thought that they're probably rehearsing their **bird songs** as they sleep, so that they'll **sing better** the next day.

Penguins in the Antarctic have to travel great distances across the ice for food, but while some penguins only waddle along, others – like the Adélie and Emperor – speed things up by **tobogganing** on their bellies, using their feet and wings to push themselves along. **Wheeeeeeeeee!**

Wheeeeeeeeeeee!

MAD
MAMMALS

Animals are not always what they seem. **Cheetahs** are fit and fast, and so athletic they can change direction **in mid-air** – but after a cheetah has caught and killed a victim, it has to **lie down** for half an hour to **catch its breath** before it can find the energy to eat.

Easy-going **dugongs**, sometimes called **sea cows**, enjoy slow and quiet days swimming in shallow seas on the eastern coast of Africa. But if there's a shark attack, the dugongs spring into action, **ganging up together** in a group and **headbutting** the shark away with their large square snouts.

Don't get too close to a **proboscis monkey**'s long and funny-looking nose. When these monkeys want to scare away enemies, they make **loud honking noises**, and their noses shoot straight out with every blast.

Moonrats from the rainforests of south–east Asia look like hedgehogs, but with fur instead of spines. They live alone and mark their dens with a liquid that smells like **rotting onions** to keep enemies and other moonrats away.

Perfect for the Secret Club, I think.

Some animals use their smells to **make friends**, like male **musk oxen** from northern Canada. They produce a **stinky liquid** from under their eyes which they rub onto trees and bushes to attract female oxen, who can pick up the smell from miles away.

Sometimes **ferrets** sleep so soundly their owners think they are **dead**. Even picking them up and shaking them doesn't wake them – they just lie like **limp rags** with their eyes shut.

When **guinea pigs** jump up and down, it's called '**popcorning**' because it looks like popcorn does when it jumps around during cooking.

Northern grasshopper mice from North America look small and sweet, but don't believe it! They love to gobble up all kinds of meat, including scorpions, tarantulas, snakes and even other mice. No wonder their nickname is **killer mice**.

Australian **wombats** are the only animals in the world that produce **cube-shaped poo**. Every morning, the wombat drops 80 to 100 cubes of poo around its burrow to mark out its territory. Guess what? The shape of the poo **stops it rolling away**.

Can you believe it? **Cows** like to **hang out** with their **friends** every day. Researchers have discovered that if a cow is taken away from its best friend it **produces less milk**, and can even get ill.

Rhinos can be a scary sight. They aim their horns at their enemies and charge head on – but because their **eyesight is bad**, they often end up attacking **trees and rocks** by mistake!

Rodents, like **squirrels**, **beavers**, and **chipmunks**, have large front teeth that **never stop growing**. But their teeth never get too big because they're **worn away** by the animals gnawing at tough plants and nuts.

Sea otters have **pockets in their skin** which they use to store **tools**! They keep rocks in these pockets which they use to crack open the hard shells of the molluscs they eat.

Giant anteaters, found in South America, can flick their long, sticky tongues **150 times a minute**.

North American **beavers** can fell large trees using nothing more than their **front teeth**. They use the logs to build dams across lakes and rivers.

Coyotes and **North American badgers** are unlikely friends, but they **join forces** to hunt for food. The coyotes sniff out the rats they both love to eat, and then the badgers dig them up – and they both take a share of the supper.

When **bats** are hungry, they don't hold back. A bat can eat **3,000** insects in just one night!

Baboons spend most of their days on the ground, but they sleep perched **high** in trees **balanced on their heels** to avoid attacks from lions, leopards and pythons.

FROGFACE
FACTOIDS

Frogs can't see colours or shapes very well, but they are brilliant at spotting anything that **moves**. Their long, sticky, **curled-up tongue** shoots out like a party blower to catch insects passing by.

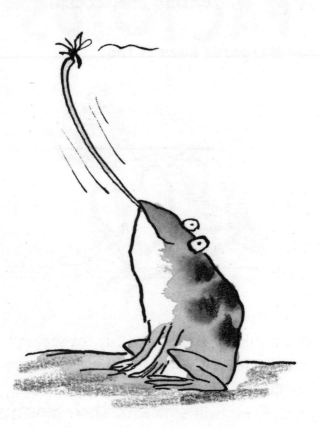

Have you ever seen a **frog** twisting and turning weirdly? If so, it was probably **shedding** its **skin**. Frogs do this about once a week, stretching themselves out of their old skin, before pulling it off over their heads like a jumper – and **eating** it. **Blecccch!**

I bet Margaret does it too.

If you think **eyeballs** are only for seeing with – you're wrong! **Frogs** also use their eyeballs to **swallow**. They gulp their food whole, then their eyeballs **sink into their mouths** and push the food down their throats.

During cold North American winters, hibernating **wood frogs** manage to survive even though up to 70% of their bodies turn to **ice** and their **hearts stop beating**. When spring comes, the frogs thaw out and leap back to life.

Ever wondered what the inside of a frog looks like? Look at a **South American glass frog** and you'll find out. Their skin is so transparent that if you turn one upside down and look at its tummy, you can see its **heart**, **liver** and **intestines** too.

No wonder **Amazon horned frogs** from Brazil are as big and round as a saucer – **they eat almost everything**. But sometimes they bite off more than they can chew. They've been found **dead** with victims too big to swallow still **sticking out of their mouths.**

Northern slimy salamanders from America produce a substance as sticky as **glue** from their skin. If snakes or turtles try to attack them, their mouths get **slimed up**, and the salamander escapes.

Frogs need water – so how do they survive in the Australian desert? **Water-holding frogs** have the answer. They spend most of the time buried a metre under the sand, emerging only after heavy rain to fill their bladders and skin pockets with water before returning underground and sealing themselves in a water-tight **cocoon of slime**.

Surinam horned frogs don't have the same problem – their mouths are so massive that they can swallow mice, rats and other frogs **whole** without any trouble.

Spatulate-nosed tree frogs from Central America have long, pointy heads, which comes in handy when the weather gets hot and dry – the frogs crawl into damp holes and **plug up** the entrances with their **big noses**.

Frogs, toads and salamanders usually eat insects, slugs and snails, but there's one type of frog that likes eating **fruit** – the **Izecksohn's treefrog** from Brazil.

RABID
REPTILES

If you're looking for a **Satanic leaf-tailed gecko**, you'll have to search the rainforest hard. These geckos' bodies look like **dead leaves** – their tails are even marked like the veins of a leaf, with edges that look as though they have been **nibbled**!

Rattlesnakes are still dangerous up to an **hour** after they have been killed. People have been bitten even after **shooting** a snake several times or **cutting off its head**.

Did you know that **turtles and tortoises** are **toothless**? They chew their way through fruit and vegetables with just their sharp beaks and strong jaws. But beware: **snapping turtles'** beaks are so strong that they can **bite through human fingers**.

Crafty **basilisk lizards** usually sleep at the very end of a branch hanging over a pond or lake. Then, if a snake tries to crawl down the branch to **grab** the lizard, the additional weight on the branch makes it move, **shaking** the lizard safely off into the water.

Marine iguanas, found on the Galapagos Islands near South America, often look as though they are wearing **white wigs**. It's actually salt – they **sneeze** it out of their noses and it lands on their heads.

Crocodiles cry, but not because they are sad. Their eyes make tears when they have been on land for a while and their eyes are beginning to **dry out**.

Shingleback skinks are a type of lizard from Australia that look as though they have **two heads**. Actually, the second head is just a large, stumpy head-shaped **tail**. They can even detach this tail to help them escape, but they only do this in emergencies because it takes about **eight months** to grow back.

If **grass snakes** are threatened, they pretend to be **dead**. They lie with their tongues hanging out and give off a **disgusting smell** to put off their attacker.

Do **pythons** make great pets? Maybe – unless they **escape**! In August 1984, there was a terrible panic in New York when a python vanished from its cage – until it was found in its owner's attic. In January 1994, in a Californian apartment building, a python escaped from its owner by crawling down the toilet, causing **chaos** among the other terrified residents.

Wouldn't that be a great trick to play on Stuck-up Steve?

CRAZY CREEPY-CRAWLIES

Scorpions are so tough they can survive a night in the freezer! Researchers have put **frozen scorpions** in the sun and watched them thaw out and **spring back to life**.

The female **burying beetle** lays her eggs near to the dead body of a small bird or rodent she has hidden, so that when the baby beetles are born they can **feast on its rotting flesh**.

Dracula ants feed on the blood of their own babies. They bring back food for their young – but when they are fat, the parents **chew holes** in the babies' skin and **suck out their blood**.

Kenyan jumping spiders are sometimes called **vampire spiders** because their favourite food is mosquitoes . . . full of human blood.

I must introduce Rabid Rebecca to some.

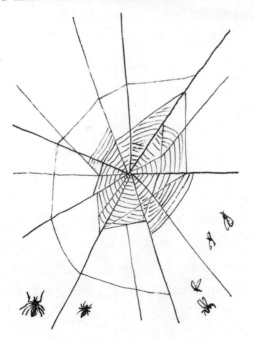

Have you heard of the weird worms that eat the bones of **dead whales** in the sea? They are known as **bone-eating snot flower worms**!

When in danger, some workers from a colony of **Malaysian exploding ants** use special muscles to **burst open** their bodies and spray out a poisonous sticky substance. The exploded ants **die** but the rest of the colony are saved.

Japanese giant hornets are large and fierce – a single hornet can kill 40 European honey bees in a minute. The hornets **dismember** the bees and return to their nest with the body parts, which they feed to their young.

Crab spiders, found in many parts of the world including Africa, China and the UK, don't build webs to catch their food. Instead they hide among plants and flowers and **lie in wait** for insects. Some of them can even change colour to match their hiding place.

When **Bombardier beetles** are in danger, they spray not one, but two horrible gases from their rear ends which mix together and make an **explosion**. How rude!

Why not keep a **Madagascan hissing cockroach**? They are easy to feed and don't bite – they even stop hissing if you **pet** them enough. But they are **good at escaping**, so experts advise coating the top of their enclosure with petroleum jelly so it's too slippery for them to climb.

If a **tarantula** loses a leg, it soon grows another. Its new leg is often shorter than the others at first, though, so the spider scuttles along with a **limp**!

FREAKY
FISH

Alligator gars of North and Central America are three-metre-long fish with scales, wide snouts and mouths **full of fangs**. Amazingly, no one has ever been attacked by one, but if you even touch one of their bright red eggs, its **poison** will make you sick.

Birds beware! **Arapaimas** are large fish that live in the rainforest rivers of South America. They lurk near the water's surface hunting for food, and sometimes **leap out of the water** to grab birds from low-hanging branches.

In North America, you might be surprised to hear a **dog barking** from the bottom of a pond. But it is more likely to be a fish called a **Mudpuppy** or **Waterdog**, which makes a noise similar to a dog.

WOOF WOOF

Swimming among the coral reefs of Australia and the Bahamas, **butterfly fish** dazzle with their bright patterns of blue, red, orange and yellow. But at night they vanish when their brilliant colours fade away to blend in with the dark water.

Herrings talk to each other by **breaking wind**! It sounds as if they are blowing a **high-pitched raspberry**. Herrings keep in contact with each other in the dark in this way, but the fish that eat them can't hear such high-pitched sounds.

Have you heard of **psychedelic frogfish**? These weird orange and white fish were first discovered in Indonesia in 2008. They are the size of a human fist and they move around by pushing themselves off from the seabed with their fins, bouncing like **rubber balls**.

Thresher sharks grow up to six metres long, and their **deadly tails** make up half of their body length. Whipping their tails through the water, they herd together schools of small fish. They stun and kill them with **vicious** blows, then they feast on the **bloodbath**.

The **ocean sunfish** looks like a **big blob**! At four metres tall and three metres wide, it is the only fish taller than it is long. Instead of scales, its round flat body is covered with a thick layer of **gooey slime**.

Nurse sharks sleep during the day on the sea floor of the Atlantic and Pacific Oceans, sometimes in groups of up to 40, all piled on top of each other.

All **barramundis**, giant Australian fish which grow to nearly two metres long (the height of a very tall man) start life as **males**. But when they reach 50 cm in length, usually at about five years old, they all **become female** and stay that way for the rest of their lives.

Nicknamed 'the **wastebasket** of the sea', **tiger sharks** will **eat almost anything**. With their sharp teeth and strong jaws, they munch their way through turtles, stingrays, seals and squid – and have even been found with **car tyres** in their stomachs.

Another creature's bottom sounds like the worst place to live, but the little **pearlfish** finds the **sea cucumber**'s bottom the ideal place to **hide from its enemies**. Sometimes they even live there in pairs, popping out only at night to find food.

STRANGE
SEA CREATURES

Beachball-sized **Dumbo octopuses** get their name from their huge pairs of fins, which look like **elephants' ears**.

Giant clams at the bottom of the Atlantic Ocean can grow to the size of **suitcases** and weigh more than 200 kg. But it takes them nearly 100 years to get that big!

Starfish can turn their stomachs inside out! If a **starfish** fancies shellfish for supper, it wraps its arms around the shell and pulls it open. Then it **pushes its stomach out of its mouth**, which oozes inside the shell and eats the seafood.

Beware **geography cones** in the waters of southeast Asia – these 15 cm killer snails are the world's most dangerous shellfish. They shoot out a **deadly weapon** like a sharp tooth, filled with venom strong enough to kill a human.

Giant cuttlefish hide from their enemies by changing colour to blend with their background. They can even **change the texture of their skin** to look like rocks, sand or seaweed.

Leafy sea dragons look like sea horses in **camouflage**. They appear to have leaves hanging off them and sprouting out of their heads – this helps them **hide** in the floating seaweed of the Australian coastline.

Octopuses have nine brains – one in their head and eight in their limbs – so all of their tentacles can **think for themselves**!

Sea cucumbers are sausage-shaped creatures that live on the seabed. If they are attacked by other fish, they **puke up** lots of sticky thread, and while the fish struggle, the slow-moving sea cucumbers escape.

Decorator crabs are well camouflaged as they scuttle along the ocean floor – they **dress up** by hanging bits of seaweed and shells on the special curved hairs on their bodies.

Limpets might look as though they never move, but every day they creep over the rocks on their one big foot, scraping up food with their tongues. They can wander up to two metres away . . . but every night they return to **exactly** the same place.

On Christmas Island near Australia, 120 million **red crabs** hide away in burrows in the rainforest. Every October, they emerge and head for the sea, scuttling along together like a **huge red wave**. They crawl over anything that gets in their way and even **stop traffic**.

MOBS, MURDERS AND BLOATS

Everyone has heard of **flocks of birds** or **swarms of insects**, but there are some really crazy names for groups of animals. Check these out.

It's said a **murder of crows** will circle round sites like battlefields and cemeteries where animals or people are expected to **die**.

By the coast, the harsh squawking of a **squabble of seagulls** can usually be heard as they **fight** over food.

Hyenas are often described as laughing. A group is called a **cackle of hyenas**, a type of laugh associated with **witches**.

How about a moody of Margarets or a sour of Susans?

Hedgehogs are the only British wild animal with spines. A group of them is called a **prickle of hedgehogs**.

Desert-dwelling **meerkats** may look cute, but they live in groups of between 20 to 50 and at dinnertime they form a menacing **mob of meerkats** as they hunt for food.

Rhinos can run at 48 km an hour, but they can't see very far. Can you imagine what could happen if a **crash of rhinos** suddenly had to stop?!

Even though they only eat grass, **hippos** are the third heaviest land animal after elephants and rhinos. They are known as a **bloat of hippos**.

A flutter of butterflies is the perfect name. When a group of butterflies fly by you, only the gentlest fluttering sound can be heard.

In the evening light, a **cloud of bats** can sometimes be seen diving for insects in the sky.

QUIRKY
QUESTIONS
& ANSWERS

Q: Are dragons real?

A: No. But the world's biggest lizards – Komodo dragons – come closest to the mythical fire-breathing ones from stories. They don't have wings or fiery breath, but they do have 60 jagged teeth up to 2.5 cm long, a ferocious bite, strong claws, and mouths dripping with venomous slime.

Q: Can mice be green?

A: Yes. In 1997, scientists in Japan took the chemical that makes some jellyfish glow-in-the-dark green and put it into mouse egg cells. The result was glowing green mice.

Q: Is the Loch Ness Monster real?

A: Who knows! When a photo of Nessie was published in the *Daily Mail* on 21st April 1934, everyone was obsessed with finding the monster. 60 years later, the photographer admitted that he had faked the picture by using wood and plastic powered by a clockwork toy submarine. Visitors still flock to Loch Ness and many claim to have caught a glimpse of the creature. Sightings have died down over the years and no real evidence has ever been found – so it may always be a mystery.

Q: Did the Kraken sea monster ever exist?

A: No. In the mid-eighteenth century, Norwegian sailors feared a great beast called the Kraken, which they believed would come up from the ocean depths, pull their ship apart and eat them one by one. But the legend most likely came from sightings of giant squid, like the one caught alive in 2007 in Antarctica which weighed half a tonne and was 14 metres long.

Q: Are zoos the best place to see wild animals?

A: Most of the time. But when two zebras died in 2009, at the Marah Land Zoo in Asia, the zoo didn't have enough money to replace them. So they painted donkeys to look like their stripy cousins, using masking tape and black hair dye!

Q: Can animals from different species ever be friends?

A: Yes. Baloo the bear, Shere Khan the tiger and Leo the lion were all rescued in 2001 when they were three months old. They grew up together at the Noah's Ark Animal Rescue Centre in Georgia, USA. They are still great friends, eating, sleeping and even play-fighting together.

Q: Are penguins ticklish?

A: Yes. In 2011, a tiny penguin called Cookie became an internet star after he had a fit of high-pitched giggles when his handler tickled him at Cincinnati Zoo in the USA.

Hee Hee

Q: What is Bigfoot?

A: In the 1950s there were reports of a mysterious, hairy beast roaming the wilderness of North America, leaving large footprints behind it. No teeth, hair or bones have ever been found, and the only evidence has been a film shot in 1967, which many people believe to be fake. In it, Bigfoot looks rather like a man wearing a gorilla suit.

Q: Do different animals ever help each other?

A: Yes. In Poland in 2010, Baks the boxer dog had an accident which left him blind. He was befriended by a goose called Buttons who today leads the dog everywhere, hanging onto him with her neck or honking to tell him which way to go. Baks's owner said that the dog and goose are inseparable and even chase the postman together.

Q: Can animals go to university?

A: Yes. When eighteenth-century poet, Lord Byron, started at Cambridge University, he was annoyed to be told he could not take his dog with him. Instead, according to some of the other students, Byron brought a tame bear, which stayed with him until he graduated.

Q: Do camel spiders actually eat camels?

A: No. During the Iraq war of 2003, there were photos of camel spiders half the size of humans, and stories of them eating camels and even soldiers. But the photos were faked, and the stories weren't true. Camel spiders are still quite scary though – the size of a man's fist, they kill rats, lizards and birds and can run at 10 miles an hour.

SLEEPIEST, SLIMIEST, SMELLIEST . . .

It's always the fastest, the biggest and the brainiest who win the awards. But what about the **sleepiest**, the **slimiest** and the **smelliest**?

Sleepiest – When it gets cold outside, **Arctic squirrels** from North America snuggle into cosy burrows and settle into a deep winter sleep for a full six months. Yawn! Even Lazy Linda couldn't sleep that long.

Slimiest – Hagfish, jawless, boneless deep-sea creatures, can produce up to eight litres of **slime** – that's four big bottles of fizzywizz – in just a few minutes when they are attacked.

Slowest swimmer – At only 2.5 cm long, **dwarf seahorses** move about 2-3 cm per minute – and that's when they are in a hurry!

Smelliest – Striped polecats from Africa, also called **zorillas**, squirt out such a **stinky** spray from under their tails that the **fumes** choke any predator. Zorillas scare off lions and leopards by simply raising their tails and threatening to spray.

Noisiest land animal – While blue whales get the award under the sea, on land the **howler monkeys** of Central and South America are the loudest. Their ear-piercing screeches echo across the forest, and they can be heard from nearly five km away.

Heaviest teeth – **Elephants** win the award for their overgrown gnashers. An old male elephant can have tusks that are up to three metres long – taller than a man – and weigh up to 100 kgs each.

Longest tooth – Narwhals from the Arctic just beat elephants for this prize because their one long tooth or tusk can be over three metres long. The tusk grows from their nose in a long point, and is spiralled like a corkscrew, giving this whale the nickname 'unicorn of the sea'.

Laziest – Sea creatures called **barnacles** attach themselves to rocks or ships when they are babies and grow a hard outer shell. Then they stay in the same place, **never moving**, for the rest of their lives.

Biggest eyes – Giant squid can see in the dark depths of the oceans with their enormous eyes, which are more than 25 cm across – the size of a **dinner plate**.

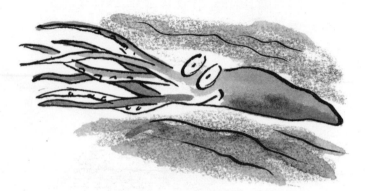

Most brainless – Jellyfish and **starfish** are joint winners, because they don't have any brains at all.

Just like Beefy Bert!

Biggest bird horn – South American **horned screamers** have a long spindly spine measuring up to 15 cm, which sticks up from their heads above their beaks.

Prickliest – **Porcupines** have more than **25,000 spines** which can be up to 30 cm long. The sharp tips stick into flesh and are painful to pull out.

Googliest eyes – Chameleons have two big bulging eyes with scaly cone-shaped eyelids. Each eye can **move on its own**, so the chameleon can look in two directions at once – perfect for spotting tasty insects to eat and keeping watch for enemies at the same time.

Bye!

HORRID HENRY BOOKS

Horrid Henry
Horrid Henry and the Secret Club
Horrid Henry Tricks the Tooth Fairy
Horrid Henry's Nits
Horrid Henry Gets Rich Quick
Horrid Henry's Haunted House
Horrid Henry and the Mummy's Curse
Horrid Henry's Revenge
Horrid Henry and the Bogey Babysitter
Horrid Henry's Stinkbomb
Horrid Henry's Underpants
Horrid Henry Meets the Queen
Horrid Henry and the Mega-Mean Time Machine
Horrid Henry and the Football Fiend
Horrid Henry's Christmas Cracker
Horrid Henry and the Abominable Snowman
Horrid Henry Robs the Bank
Horrid Henry Wakes the Dead
Horrid Henry Rocks
Horrid Henry and the Zombie Vampire
Horrid Henry's Monster Movie
Horrid Henry's Nightmare
Horrid Henry's Krazy Ketchup

Early Readers
Don't Be Horrid, Henry!
Horrid Henry's Birthday Party
Horrid Henry's Holiday
Horrid Henry's Underpants
Horrid Henry Gets Rich Quick
Horrid Henry and the Football Fiend
Horrid Henry's Nits
Horrid Henry and Moody Margaret
Horrid Henry's Thank You Letter
Horrid Henry Reads a Book
Horrid Henry's Car Journey
Moody Margaret's School
Horrid Henry Tricks and Treats

Visit Horrid Henry's website at **www.horridhenry.co.uk**
for competitions, games, downloads and a monthly newsletter.

the orion star

CALLING ALL GROWN-UPS!
Sign up for **the orion star** newsletter to
hear about your favourite authors and exclusive
competitions, plus details of how children
can join our 'Story Stars' review panel.

Sign up at:

www.orionbooks.co.uk/orionstar